How Can I HELP?

A Book about Caring

ROBIN NELSON

Lerner Publications Company • Minneapolis

Lerner Publications Company
A division of Lerner Publishing Group, Inc.
241 First Avenue North
Minneapolis, MN 55401 U.S.A.

For reading levels and more information, look up this title
at www.lernerbooks.com.

Library of Congress Cataloging-in-Publication Data

Nelson, Robin, 1971–
       How can I help? : a book about caring / by Robin Nelson.
         pages   cm. — (Show your character)
       Includes index.
       ISBN 978–1–4677–1365–8 (lib. bdg. : alk. paper)
       ISBN 978–1–4677–2524–8 (eBook)
       1. Helping behavior in children—Juvenile literature. 2. Caring in
children—Juvenile literature. I. Title.
       BF723.H45N45 2014
       177'.7—dc22   2013013616

Manufactured in the United States of America
1 – MG – 12/31/13

TABLE OF CONTENTS

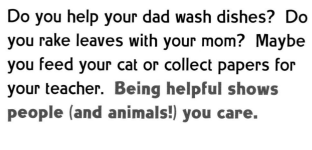

Do you help your dad wash dishes? Do you rake leaves with your mom? Maybe you feed your cat or collect papers for your teacher. **Being helpful shows people (and animals!) you care.**

Caring means feeling or showing concern for other people. You can show others you care in many ways. Be kind. Help those who need it. Always think of other people's feelings. Never be mean.

You may not always feel like helping. But **helping others makes them feel happy.** It makes you feel happy too! How can you help and show you care? There are many answers to that question. We'll show you a few of them!

The boy who sits next to me at school doesn't have any crayons, glue, or scissors. He looks sad.

HOW CAN I HELP SOMEONE WHO DOESN'T HAVE WHAT HE NEEDS?

Share your supplies with him. Sharing will show him you care.

You don't know why he doesn't have any school supplies. Maybe he forgot them. Maybe his parents were too busy to buy them. Or maybe they can't afford them.

You could ask your parents to buy some extra supplies. Take the extra supplies to your teacher. You could also **donate** them to your school for other kids who need them.

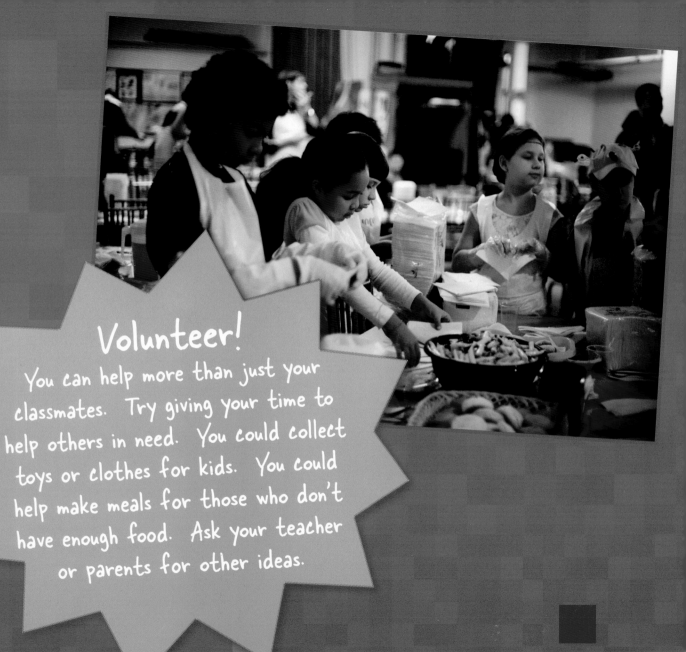

Volunteer!

You can help more than just your classmates. Try giving your time to help others in need. You could collect toys or clothes for kids. You could help make meals for those who don't have enough food. Ask your teacher or parents for other ideas.

Teasing and pushing is bullying. Bullying is not okay. But it's also not okay to just watch someone get bullied.

There are things you can do to help! **Be a friend** to Wes. Ask him to walk with you in the hall. The older kids may be less likely to bully him if he isn't alone. You could also **tell the kids to stop**. If you're not comfortable doing that, then **tell an adult**. A teacher or your mom or dad can help you handle the situation.

If the bully won't stop, talk to an adult.

9

The new girl in our class is sitting all by herself at lunch. **HOW DO I MAKE SOMEONE FEEL INCLUDED?**

Starting a new school is hard. She is probably feeling lonely. Walk over to her and **invite her to sit with you**. Introduce her to your friends.

But what if she doesn't want to sit with us?

Then you could sit with her at lunch today and **get to know her one-on-one**. Maybe once she knows you, she'll want to meet your friends too.

Inviting someone to join you is a great way to show you care.

Dan is a boy in my class. He was in the hospital and has missed a lot of school. **CAN I HELP MY CLASSMATE AND CHEER HIM UP?**

Yes! You and your class could **make him cards**. Looking at messages and pictures his friends made may make him feel better. Your class could even make a video for him to watch.

You could bring Dan his homework. Ask his mom or dad if you can see him. If he's feeling well enough, you could **help him with his homework**. And he would probably love a visit.

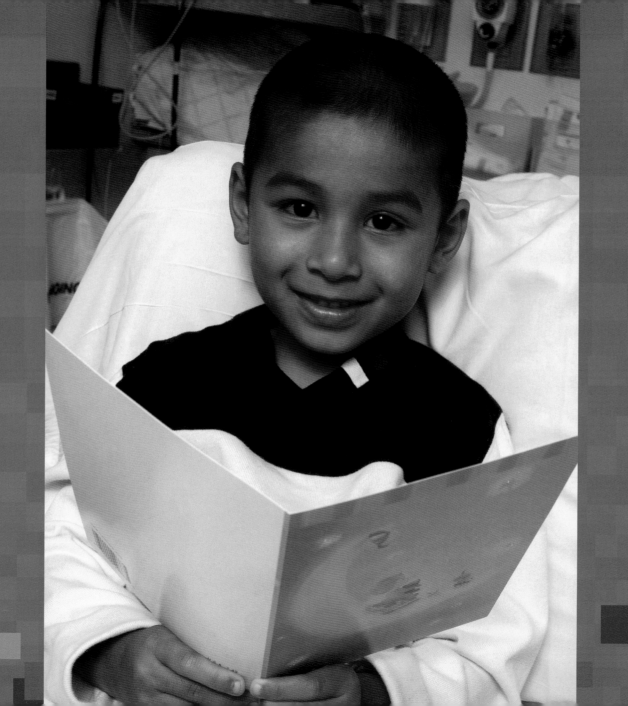

My friend Ashley looks sad. She doesn't smile or laugh at my jokes. She didn't say anything at lunch. She doesn't want to play at recess.

WHAT CAN I DO TO MAKE MY FRIEND FEEL BETTER?

Ask Ashley what's wrong. **Be a good listener** if she wants to talk. If she doesn't want to talk, tell her that's okay. Just be her friend. Give Ashley a hug. Hugs often make people feel better.

If Ashley still seems sad after a couple of weeks, tell an adult. Your teacher or one of your parents may be able to help her.

Being there for a friend is a great way to show you care.

My great-grandma lives in a nursing home. My mom wants me to visit her. I love my great-grandma, but the nursing home makes me uncomfortable.

SHOULD I VISIT MY GREAT-GRANDMA AT THE NURSING HOME?

Visiting your great-grandma would be a good way to show her you care.

First, talk to your mom about why you are worried about seeing your great-grandma. Maybe it's because she doesn't remember you. Maybe it's all the strange sights and smells at the nursing home. Whatever it is, **think about how much your great-grandma will love seeing you**.

What will I do with my great-grandma at the nursing home?

Bring your great-grandma something you made yourself. You could **draw her a picture**. Or you could ask a parent to help bake her cookies. Tell her about what you made for her.

Bring old photos of you and your great-grandma to share with her. Great-grandparents often love to look at old pictures.

Play a game with your great-grandma. Bring one of your favorite board games and teach her how to play. Maybe she could teach you a card game.

Whatever you do, it's important to visit your great-grandma to show her you love her and care for her.

19

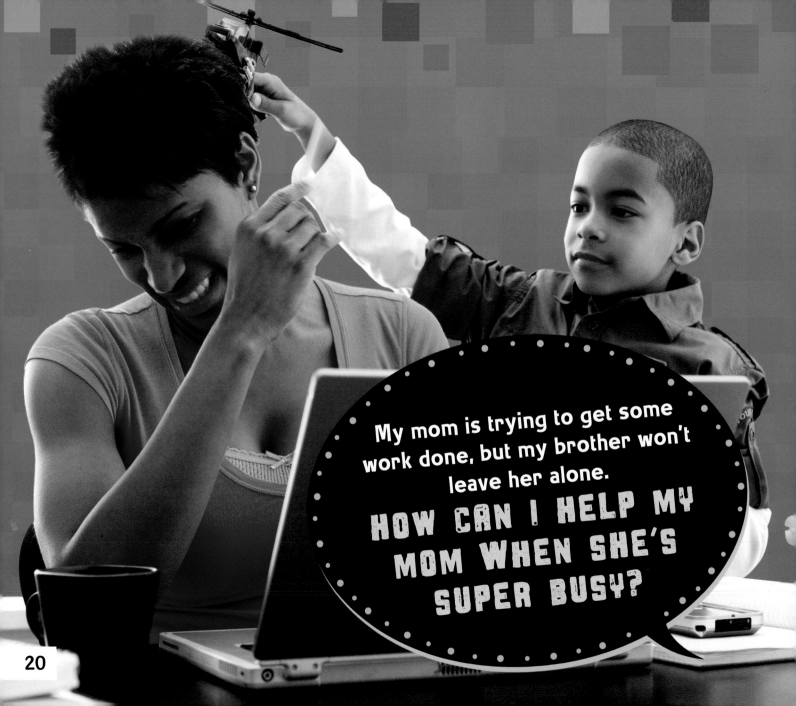

My mom is trying to get some work done, but my brother won't leave her alone.

HOW CAN I HELP MY MOM WHEN SHE'S SUPER BUSY?

20

Play with your brother. He will love that you are spending time with him. And your mom will be happy to get her work done. Do something you and your brother will both enjoy. You could play with him outside or share your toys.

We got a lot of snow last night. My neighbor is older and has a hard time walking. I'm worried he might fall or hurt himself shoveling.

IS THERE ANYTHING I CAN DO TO SHOW MY NEIGHBOR I CARE?

You could bundle up and **shovel your neighbor's sidewalk**. Won't he be surprised and happy when he sees his sidewalk all cleared of snow?

If you're not sure you can shovel the snow by yourself, you could see if a family member or a friend can help you.

More Ways to Be a Caring Neighbor

If you aren't able to shovel, you could bring your neighbor's mail to him instead. That way, he doesn't have to walk to the mailbox. Or you could spread sand on icy patches so he doesn't slip. Another great thing to do is to offer to help him if you see he's having difficulty with chores or with getting around.

23

Ask your dad what you can do to help him. Could you pick up your toys? Could you feed the cat? Maybe you could put books back on the bookshelf. What about playing with your little sister while your dad works?

Helping around the house will show your dad you care. And then your dad will have more time to play with you.

Spend time with your mom on her birthday. Do some of her favorite things. You can also make your mom a card. Write down the things you love about her. And don't forget to give her lots of hugs!

It's wonderful to show your family and friends you care. But **don't stop there**. It's easy and fun to help others too. What can you do to show people you care?

RANDOM ACTS OF KINDNESS

Do you need some ideas to show people you care? Check out this list!

1. Smile and say "Hello!"

2. Hold the door open for someone.

3. Say something nice to someone, like "Great job!"

4. Collect food for a food shelf.

5. Write a thank-you note to your teacher.

6. Draw a picture for your bus driver.

7. Pick up trash on the playground or at a park.

8. Call your grandparents just to say hi.

9. Tell your parents you love them.

10. Invite a new friend over to play.

bullying: making someone feel hurt, afraid, or uncomfortable over and over again

caring: feeling or showing concern for other people

donate: to give something to help other people

helpful: willing to help someone to do a job or deal with a problem

nursing home: a place where some people who are older or who have special needs live and are taken care of

FURTHER INFORMATION

Donovan, Sandy. *How Can I Deal with Bullying? A Book about Respect.* Minneapolis: Lerner Publications, 2014. Read about bullying and how to deal with it.

Espeland, Pamela. *Helping Out and Staying Safe: The Empowerment Assets.* Minneapolis: Free Spirit Publishing, 2004. Learn simple, everyday ways you can be helpful in your home and community.

Giving & Me
http://learningtogive.org/students/giving_and_me/#home
Try fun activities to learn about giving time and money to help others.

Kids Are Heroes
http://kidsareheroes.org
Visit this site to learn all about everyday heroes who are helping others.

Kindness Ideas
http://www.kindspring.org/ideas.php
Want to do something caring but don't know what to do? Visit this site for lots of ideas!

Prokos, Anna. *Helping Hands.* South Egremont, MA: Red Chair Press, 2010. Who will help Ocho the Octopus when he needs it?

INDEX

PHOTO ACKNOWLEDGMENTS

The images in this book are used with the permission of: © Szefei/Dreamstime.com, p. 4; © KidStock/Blend Images/Getty Images, p. 5; © iStockphoto.com/kwanisik , p. 6; © Richard Levine/Alamy, p. 7; © David Roth/ Stone/Getty Images, p. 8; © Marsia16/Dreamstime.com, p. 9; © Monkey Business Images/Dreamstime.com, pp. 11, 18; © Newstockimages/SuperStock, p. 13; © Kevin Dodge/Radius Images/Getty Images, pp. 14, 15; © James Steidl/SuperFusion/SuperStock, p. 17; © Fuse/Thinkstock, pp. 19, 23; © Radius/SuperStock, p. 20; © Blend Images/Thinkstock, p. 21; © Intst/Dreamstime.com, p. 22; © JGI/Jamie Grill/Blend Images/Getty Images, p. 24; © Jupiterimages/Creatas/Thinkstock, p. 25; © Jon Feingersh/Blend Images/Getty Images, p. 26; © Get4net/Dreamstime.com, p. 27; © Yurolaitsalbert/Dreamstime.com, p.29.

Front Cover: © Leland Bobbé/CORBIS.

Main body text set in ChurchwardSamoa Regular. Typeface provided by Chank.